© **Haynes Publishing 2007**

This book is officially licensed by Winning Moves UK Ltd,
owners of the Top Trumps registered trademark.

Peter March has asserted his right to be identified as the
author of this book.

British Library Cataloguing-in-Publication Data:
A catalogue record for this book is available from the British
Library

ISBN 978 1 84425 416 3

Library of Congress catalog card no. 2006936110

Published by Haynes Publishing,
Sparkford, Yeovil, Somerset BA22 7JJ, UK
Tel: 01963 442030 Fax: 01963 440001
Int. tel: +44 1963 442030 Int. fax: +44 1963 440001
Email: sales@haynes.co.uk
Website: www.haynes.co.uk

Haynes North America, Inc.,
861 Lawrence Drive, Newbury Park
California 91320, USA

Printed and bound in Great Britain by
J. H. Haynes & Co. Ltd, Sparkford

Photographic credits:

All photographs courtesy PRM Aviation Collection

The Author

Peter March is one of the UK's leading aviation experts. He has written
for and edited several leading aviation magazines, and has more than 100
books on military and civil aviation to his credit.

R87642

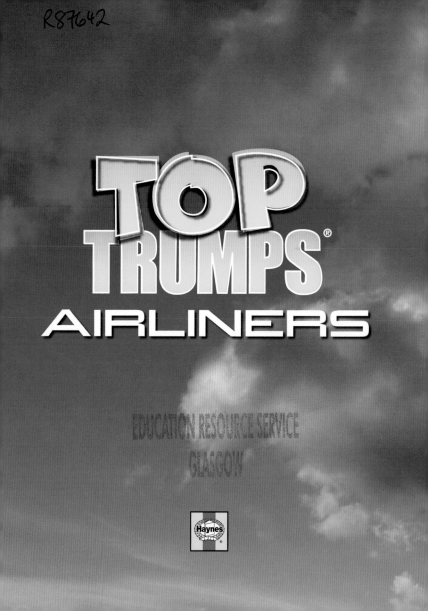

TOP TRUMPS®

AIRLINERS

Haynes

Contents

Introduction	6
Aérospatiale/BAC • Concorde	8
Airbus • A300	12
Airbus • A320	16
Airbus • A330	20
Airbus • A340	24
Airbus • A380	28
Antonov • An-24	32
Avions de Transport Regional • ATR 42	36
Boeing • 707	40
Boeing • 727	44
Boeing • 737	48
Boeing • 747	52
Boeing • 757	56
Boeing • 767	60
Boeing • 777	64
Bombardier/Canadair • CRJ	68
Bombardier/DHC • Dash 8	72
British Aerospace • BAe 146/Avro RJ	76
British Aerospace • Jetstream 31	80
British Aerospace • Jetstream 41	84
Britten-Norman • Islander	88
CASA • 212	92

De Havilland Canada • Twin Otter	96
Dornier • 328	100
Douglas • DC-3 Dakota	104
Douglas • DC-4 Skymaster	108
Douglas • DC-8	112
Embraer • Brasilia	116
Embraer • ERJ-145	120
Embraer • E170	124
Fairchild/Swearingen • Metro	128
Fokker • F.27 Friendship	132
Fokker • F.28 Fellowship	136
Ilyushin • Il-86	140
Let • L-410 Turbolet	144
Lockheed • TriStar	148
McDonnell Douglas • DC-9	152
McDonnell Douglas • MD-80	156
McDonnell Douglas • DC-10	160
McDonnell Douglas • MD-11	164
Saab • 340	168
Saab • 2000	172
Shorts • 360	176
Tupolev • Tu-154	180
Yakovlev • Yak-42	184
Checklist	188

W/D

About
Top Trumps

It's now more than 30 years since Britain's kids first caught the Top Trumps craze. The game remained hugely popular until the 1990s, when it slowly drifted into obscurity. Then, in 1999, UK games company Winning Moves discovered it, bought it, dusted it down, gave it a thorough makeover and introduced it to a whole new generation. And so the Top Trumps legend continues.

Nowadays, there are Top Trumps titles for just about everyone, with subjects about animals, cars, ships, aircraft and all the great films and TV shows. Top Trumps is now even more popular than before. In Britain, a pack of Top Trumps is bought every six seconds! And it's not just British children who love the game. Children in Australasia, the Far East, the Middle East, all over Europe and in North America can buy Top Trumps at their local shops.

Today you can even play the game on the internet, interactive DVD, your games console and even your mobile phone.

You've played the game...

Now read the book!

Haynes Publishing and Top Trumps have teamed up to bring you this exciting new Top Trumps book, in which you will find even more pictures, details and statistics.

Top Trumps: Airliners features 45 of the world's passenger aircraft, from the Douglas DC-3, the first 'true' airliner, to the gigantic new Airbus A380 'superjumbo' and the immortal Concorde. Packed with fascinating facts, stunning photographs and all the vital statistics, this is the essential pocket guide. And if you're lucky enough to spot any of these aircraft, then at the back of the book we've provided space for you to record when and where you saw them.

Look out for other Top Trumps books from Haynes Publishing – even more facts, even more fun!

Aérospatiale/BAC

Concorde

Four afterburning turbojet, supersonic airliner

Aérospatiale/BAC
Concorde
Four afterburning turbojet, supersonic airliner

In 1962, the British and French Governments signed an agreement to produce a supersonic airliner. Developed jointly by Aérospatiale and the British Aircraft Corporation, Concorde was a huge technological challenge. The French prototype 001 first flew on 2 March 1969, followed by the British 002 on 9 April 1969. The Russians had already flown their very similar Tupolev Tu-144 on 31 December 1968, but unlike Concorde, it was not a success. Many airlines showed interest in Concorde, but only Air France and British Airways placed orders, for a total of 16 aircraft. Capable of twice the speed of sound, Concordes operated mainly on the Atlantic route. A 'machometer' in the cabin allowed passengers to see how fast they were travelling. Concorde's four Olympus engines were mounted in pairs under the sleek delta wings, and its unusual 'droop-snoot' allowed the nose to be lowered before landing to give the pilot better visibility. Although operations continued after the crash of an Air France Concorde near Paris in July 2000, the withdrawal of the fleet was announced in April 2003. The last Concorde flight took place on 26 November that year and all surviving Concordes are now in museums or on public display.

Aérospatiale/BAC Concorde

Engines	**Four Rolls-Royce/SNECMA Olympus 593 Mk 610 afterburning turbojets**
Power	**38,050lb thrust**
Span	**25.56m (83ft 10in)**
Length	**62.10m (203ft 9in)**
Height	**11.4m (37ft 5in)**
Max weight	**185,065kg (408,000lb)**
Max cruise speed	**Mach 2.04, 2,179km/h (1,354 mph)**
Ceiling	**18,290m (60,000ft)**
Range	**5,110km (3,180 miles)**
Flight deck crew	**Three**
Passengers	**100 (144 economy)**
First flown	**2 March 1969**
Into service	**26 January 1976**

Airbus
A300

Medium-range, wide-body, twin-turbofan airliner series

Airbus A310

Airbus
A300

Medium-range, wide-body, twin-turbofan airliner series

Airbus A310

The A300 was the first design to emerge from Airbus Industrie, a European consortium formed in the late 1960s. It was designed to compete with the American wide-bodied DC-10 and TriStar airliners. The first production A300-B2 entered service with Air France in 1974. Although final assembly took place in France, large components manufactured in the UK and Germany were flown to Toulouse using an outsize transport. A total of 249 A300-B2/B4s was built before production switched to the A300-600. This had a two-crew 'glass' cockpit and could carry more passengers. First flown in April 1982 and ordered by Lufthansa, the A310 was a shorter-fuselage, smaller-capacity, longer-range version, with seating for up to 230 passengers. The A310-300, introduced into service by Swissair in 1986, was able to fly further than any of the A300 versions. Around 400 A300s and 200 A310s remain in airline service worldwide. Federal Express operates a large fleet of A300-600F freighters, and many older A300s have also been converted to carry cargo. The A300 formed the basis for the Beluga outsize transporter.

Airbus A300-600

Engines	**Two General Electric CF6-80C2A1 (or CF6-80C2A5) or two Pratt & Whitney PW4156 (or PW4158) turbofans**
Power	**61,600lb thrust**
Span	**44.84m (147ft 1in)**
Length	**54.08m (177ft 5in)**
Height	**16.62m (54ft 6.5in)**
Max weight	**170,500kg (375,855lb)**
Top speed	**897km/h (557mph)**
Cruising speed	**875km/h (544mph)**
Ceiling	**12,192m (40,000ft)**
Range	**7,540km (4,685 miles)**
Flight deck crew	**Two**
Passengers	**360**
First flown	**28 October 1972 (A300B1)**
Into service	**23 May 1974 (A300B2)**

Airbus A310

Airbus A300

Airbus
A320

Twin-turbofan, short/medium-range airliner series

Airbus A319

Airbus
A320

Twin-turbofan, short/medium-range airliner series

Airbus A318

The A320 series, which includes the A318, A319, A320 and A321, is the world's best selling single-aisle aircraft family. The A320 entered service with Air France in March 1988. It was the first airliner to introduce 'fly-by-wire' technology, enabling the pilot to control the aircraft electronically from a computerised flight deck. US airline JetBlue Airways is currently the largest operator, with a fleet of 93 A320-200s. The stretched A321 first flew in March 1993. It is 6.93m longer than the A320 and can seat up to 220 passengers. The shorter A319, which seats up to 140 passengers, has the same cockpit layout as both the A320 and A321, making it easy for airlines to operate mixed fleets. Developed as a regional airliner, the A318 is the smallest member of the Airbus family and first flew in January 2002. Powered by new Pratt & Whitney PW6000 turbofans, the A318 can carry 100 passengers. With more than 4,700 of the family ordered, and 2,900 delivered to 180 operators worldwide, the A320 series had flown 50 million hours by the end of 2006.

Airbus A320-200

Engines	**Two CFM International CFM56-5A1 (or -5A3/-5B4) or two International Aero Engines IAE V2500-A1 (or -A5) turbofans**
Power	**27,400lb thrust**
Span	**33.91m (111ft 3in)**
Length	**37.57m (123ft 3in)**
Height	**11.80m (38ft 9in)**
Max weight	**77,000kg (169,755lb)**
Top speed	**903km/h (561mph)**
Cruising speed	**840km/h (522mph)**
Ceiling	**11,277m (37,000ft)**
Range	**5,676km (3,527 miles)**
Flight deck crew	**Two**
Passengers	**179**
First flown	**22 February 1987**
Into service	**March 1988**

Airbus A318

Airbus A320

Airbus
A330

Medium/long-range, twin-turbofan, wide-body airliner

HB-IQP

Airbus
A330

Medium/long-range, twin-turbofan, wide-body airliner

With the long-range airliner market dominated by the US in the 1980s, Airbus produced the A330 to compete directly with Boeing's 747, 767 and 777 airliners. It was developed together with the four-engined A340, with which it shares many common features. Significantly, the A330 and A340 were the first airliners designed entirely by computer. The A330 follows the earlier Airbus designs in having a 'fly-by-wire' control system and digital flight deck, with extensive use of composite materials. There are two main versions, the standard A330-300 and the extended range A330-200, which is 4.7m shorter and has an extended tail fin. Although it carries fewer passengers, the -200 can fly longer routes because it has additional fuel capacity. Over half of the 400+ A330s produced so far have been delivered to airlines in Asia, the Middle East and Australasia. Hong Kong-based Cathay Pacific Airways currently operates a total of 26 A330-300s, and China Airlines, Dragonair and Qatar Airways also have substantial fleets. By early 2007, A330s had flown over five million hours with 60 different operators.

Airbus A330-200

Engines	**Two General Electric CF6-80E1A3 or two Pratt & Whitney PW4168A or two Rolls-Royce Trent 772 turbofans**
Power	**68,000–72,000lb thrust**
Span	**60.30m (197ft 10in)**
Length	**59.00m (193ft 7in)**
Height	**17.9m (58ft 9in)**
Max weight	**230,000kg (507,050lb)**
Top speed	**880km/h (547mph)**
Cruising speed	**860km/h (534mph)**
Ceiling	**12,496m (41,000ft)**
Range	**11,850km (7,363 miles)**
Flight deck crew	**Two**
Passengers	**up to 406**
First flown	**2 November 1992**
Into service	**January 1994**

Airbus
A340

Very long-range, four-turbofan, wide-body airliner

The four-engined A340 is flown on some of the world's longest and busiest routes. It was produced in parallel with the A330 in the early 1990s and is designed for intercontinental travel. Its fuselage, tail fin, undercarriage and flight deck are the same as the A330's, with modified wings to accommodate the two extra engines. The main production version is the A340-300, operated by many of the major European airlines. Due to its weight, an extra twin-wheel main landing gear is fitted under the fuselage. The extended-range A340-200 is available for long-haul routes. It first flew in April 1992 and has a shorter fuselage. The A340-500 is 3.2m longer than the -300 and can seat up to 313 passengers. Powered by four Rolls-Royce Trent turbofans, it has the longest range of any airliner in service in 2006 and can fly from New York to Singapore non-stop in 18 hours. With a fuselage stretch of 10.9m, the A340-600 version can carry the same number of passengers as the Boeing 747-400, with twice the cargo capacity. Virgin Atlantic Airways, Lufthansa and Iberia are the main operators of A340s in Europe, and a total of 370 A340s had been ordered by late 2006.

Statistics

Airbus A340-300

Engines	**Four CFM International CFM56-5C4/P turbofans**
Power	**34,000lb thrust**
Span	**60.30m (197ft 10in)**
Length	**63.6m (208ft 10in)**
Height	**16.85m (55ft 3in)**
Max weight	**275,000kg (606,000lb)**
Top speed	**914km/h (568mph)**
Cruising speed	**880km/h (547mph)**
Ceiling	**12,500m (41,000ft)**
Range	**13,700km (8,513 miles)**
Flight deck crew	**Two**
Passengers	**440**
First flown	**25 October 1991**
Into service	**March 1993**

985m

CAT II/III

Airbus
A380

Ultra long-range, four-turbofan, wide-body airliner

The rapid growth in air travel during the 1990s, together with increased traffic at airports, led Airbus to develop the four-engined A380, the world's largest airliner. It has a very spacious twin-deck cabin, capable of seating up to 555 passengers. With new generation engines and advanced wing design, the A380 is quieter and more economical than existing large airliners. Despite its size, the A380 is of conventional design and uses the latest advances in construction methods and materials. Its undercarriage is made up of 22 wheels to spread the aircraft's weight evenly when landing. The flight deck has eight large liquid crystal display (LCD) screens on the instrument panel and a head-up display (HUD) to assist the flight crew during take-off and landing. The large size of the A380 has required a number of major international airports to make big changes to be able to handle the new airliner when it enters service. Problems with the installation of the A380's 500km of wiring and other technical difficulties delayed the 'giant's' entry into service with Singapore Airlines. Orders for the A380 totalled 175 by early 2007.

Statistics

Airbus A380-800

Engines	Four Rolls-Royce Trent RB-970 or four Engine Alliance GP7270 turbofans
Power	70,000lb thrust (RB-970) 76,500lb thrust (GP7270)
Span	79.8m (261ft 8in)
Length	72.75m (238ft 7in)
Height	24.08m (79ft 7in)
Max weight	560,000kg (1,234,800lb)
Top speed	955km/h (595mph)
Cruising speed	900km/h (560mph)
Ceiling	13,100m (42,980ft)
Range	15,000km (9,321 miles)
Flight deck crew	Two
Passengers	555
First flown	27 April 2005
Into service	October 2007

Antonov
An-24

Short-range, twin-turboprop regional airliner series

An-26

405

100000

Antonov
An-24

Short-range, twin-turboprop regional airliner series

An-24

The Antonov An-24 was produced as a turboprop replacement for the earlier generation piston-engined Ilyushin Il-14s operated in large numbers in the 1950s by Aeroflot, the Russian state airline. First flown in 1959, the high-wing An-24 could seat 44 passengers on regional services. This increased to 50 when production switched to the An-24V variant. This had water-injected Ivchenko AI-24 turboprops that allowed the An-24 to operate in 'hot and high' conditions from airfields up to 3,000m above sea level. The An-24 became the most numerous type in Aeroflot service and was exported to many East European and African airlines such as Balkan Bulgarian, Egyptair, Interflug, LOT and Tarom. It remained in production for 15 years and was also developed as a freighter with an upward-hinging door at the rear of the aircraft. Production of the similar An-26 began in 1969. This version is primarily used by cargo or military operators, the main difference being its 'beaver-tail' two-position rear door arrangement to allow either ramp loading of vehicles or cargo from flat-bed ground vehicles. Nearly 1,000 An-24/26s were built before production ended in 1978.

Statistics

Antonov An-24	
Engines	Two Ivchenko AI-24VT turboprops
Power	5,060shp
Span	29.20 (95ft 10in)
Length	23.8m (78ft 1in)
Height	8.32m (27ft 4in)
Max weight	21,000kg (46,300lb)
Top speed	500km/h (310mph)
Cruising speed	450km/h (280mph)
Ceiling	8,400m (27,560ft)
Range	2,400km (1,491 miles)
Flight deck crew	Three
Passengers	50
First flown	20 December 1959 (prototype)
Into service	September 1963 (An-24)

Avions de Transport Regional

ATR 42

Twin-turboprop regional airliner series

Avions de Transport Regional
ATR 42

Twin-turboprop regional airliner series

ATR 42

Avions de Transport Regional is a joint French and Italian company set up in the early 1980s by aircraft manufacturers Aérospatiale and Alenia to develop a new regional airliner. The 42-seat ATR 42 first flew in August 1984 and entered airline service in late 1985. The main production variant was the ATR 42-300, with improved range and increased take-off weight. Uprated engines on later versions allowed 'hot and high' operations. Deliveries of the more powerful ATR 42-500 began in 1995. This version had a new cabin and six-bladed propellers that increased cruising speed. Finnish airline Kar Air became the first operator of the larger-capacity ATR 72 in October 1989. The fuselage of the ATR 72 is 4.5m longer than the ATR 42, with new wings partly built from composite materials. Popular with US airlines, American Eagle (Executive) is currently the largest operator of the type, with a fleet of 29 ATR 72s. Both types remain in production, with 312 ATR 42s and 297 ATR 72s delivered by late 2006.

Statistics

ATR 72

Engines	Two Pratt & Whitney Canada PW-127F turboprops
Power	2,750shp
Span	27.03m (88ft 9in)
Length	27.17m (89ft 2in)
Height	7.65m (25ft 1in)
Max weight	22,000kg (48,501lb)
Top speed	526km/h (327mph)
Cruising speed	460km/h (286mph)
Ceiling	7,600m (24,900ft)
Range	2,665 km (1,656 miles)
Flight deck crew	Two
Passengers	68
First flown	16 Aug 1984 (ATR 42); 27 October 1988 (ATR 72)
Into service	9 December 1985 (ATR 42); 27 October 1989 (ATR 72)

ATR 42

ATR 42

Boeing
707
Medium/long-range four-jet airliner

Boeing
707

Medium/long-range four-jet airliner

Although it came after the jet-powered Comet and Tupolev Tu-104 airliners in the early 1950s, the four-engined Boeing 707 revolutionised air travel. It brought the 'jet age' to airline passengers. Built as a private venture, the 707-80 prototype (known as the 'Dash Eighty') soon showed its military and civil potential. It was first flown in 1954, and the airliner entered service with Pan American World Airways four years later, flying on the New York to London route. The swept-wing Boeing 707 was faster, more economical, roomier and could carry more passengers over longer distances than any other airliners of the time. Boeing soon had a big order book from airlines around the world. The 707 remained in production for over 20 years and more than 900 were built, including 154 shorter fuselage, medium-range Boeing 720s. Due to noise restrictions today, most of the 707s still flying have been converted to carry cargo, operating mainly in Africa and Asia. Also developed for the US Air Force, a total of 820 of the similar KC-135 tanker was built, many of them remaining in service today.

Statistics

Boeing 707-320B

Engines	Four Pratt & Whitney JT3D-3B turbofans
Power	18,000lb thrust
Span	44.42m (145ft 9in)
Length	46.61m (152ft 11in)
Height	12.93m (42ft 5in)
Max weight	151,956kg (335,000lb)
Top speed	1,009km/h (627 mph)
Cruising speed	974km/h (605mph)
Ceiling	10,975m (36,000ft)
Range	9,913km (6,160 miles)
Flight deck crew	Four
Passengers	189
First flown	15 July 1954
Into service	26 October 1958

Boeing
727

Short/medium-range, narrow-body, tri-turbofan airliner

Boeing
727

Short/medium-range, narrow-body, tri-turbofan airliner

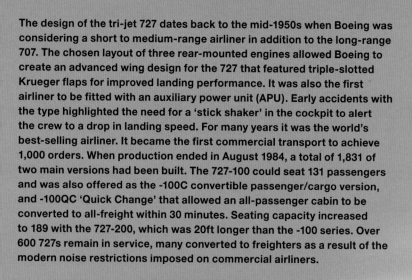

The design of the tri-jet 727 dates back to the mid-1950s when Boeing was considering a short to medium-range airliner in addition to the long-range 707. The chosen layout of three rear-mounted engines allowed Boeing to create an advanced wing design for the 727 that featured triple-slotted Krueger flaps for improved landing performance. It was also the first airliner to be fitted with an auxiliary power unit (APU). Early accidents with the type highlighted the need for a 'stick shaker' in the cockpit to alert the crew to a drop in landing speed. For many years it was the world's best-selling airliner. It became the first commercial transport to achieve 1,000 orders. When production ended in August 1984, a total of 1,831 of two main versions had been built. The 727-100 could seat 131 passengers and was also offered as the -100C convertible passenger/cargo version, and -100QC 'Quick Change' that allowed an all-passenger cabin to be converted to all-freight within 30 minutes. Seating capacity increased to 189 with the 727-200, which was 20ft longer than the -100 series. Over 600 727s remain in service, many converted to freighters as a result of the modern noise restrictions imposed on commercial airliners.

Boeing Advanced 727-200

Engines	**Three Pratt & Whitney JT8D-17 turbofans**
Power	**17,400lb thrust**
Span	**32.92m (108ft 0in)**
Length	**46.69m (153ft 2in)**
Height	**10.36m (34ft 0in)**
Max weight	**95,027kg (209,500lb)**
Top speed	**964km/h (599mph)**
Cruising speed	**917km/h (570mph)**
Ceiling	**10,210m (33,500ft)**
Range	**3,965km (2,464 miles)**
Flight deck crew	**Three**
Passengers	**189**
First flown	**9 February 1963 (prototype)**
Into service	**9 February 1964 (727-100)**

Boeing
737

Twin-turbofan, short/medium-range, narrow-body airliner series

Boeing 737-700

Boeing
737

Twin-turbofan, short/medium-range, narrow-body airliner series

Boeing 737-800

The Boeing 737 is by far the world's most successful airliner, with over 5,000 currently in service or on order. It first appeared in 1967 as the smallest capacity jet in the Boeing 'family', with seating for 100 passengers. More than half of the 737-100's structure and systems were the same as the Boeing 727, and it also had the same fuselage cross-section. The stretched 737-200 remained in production until August 1988. Second-generation 737s were introduced with the 737-300 (1984), the stretched -400 (1988), and the shorter -500 (1989) that replaced the earlier -200 series. Powered by new CFM56 turbofans, the oval-shaped engine nacelles (outer casings) made these versions very different in appearance from early 737s. In December 1997, the Next Generation 737-700 entered service, followed by the -600 a year later. These have longer wings with greater chord and area, larger tail surfaces and digital 'glass' flight decks. The most advanced 737s are the extended fuselage -800 and -900 series, the latter with increased seating for up to 189. The -800 is the highest-selling version of the 737, with 249 on order or delivered to Irish airline Ryanair. The latest version of the aircraft, the Extended Range 737-900ER, first flew on 5 September 2006.

Statistics

Boeing 737-800

Engines	**Two CFM International CFM56-7 turbofans**
Power	**26,290lb thrust**
Span	**34.31m (112ft 7in)**
Length	**39.47m (129ft 6in)**
Height	**12.56m (41ft 2in)**
Max weight	**78,240kg (172,519lb)**
Top speed	**974km/h (605mph)**
Cruising speed	**938km/h (583mph)**
Ceiling	**12,496m (41,000ft)**
Range	**5,440km (3,380 miles)**
Flight deck crew	**Two**
Passengers	**162**
First flown	**9 April 1967 (737-100)**
Into service	**10 February 1968 (737-100)**

AIR MALTA

9H-ABT

Boeing 737-300

Boeing
747

Four-turbofan, long-range, wide-body airliner

Boeing
747

Four-turbofan, long-range, wide-body airliner

As with the Boeing 707 15 years earlier, the first flight of the 747 in 1969 was an important event in the history of aviation. It made economic international air travel possible for millions of people. Much larger and heavier than other airliners at the time, the 747 quickly earned the nickname 'Jumbo Jet'. Its most notable feature is the distinctive 'hump' over the forward fuselage housing the flight deck and upper passenger cabin. An initial order for 25 747s was placed by Pan Am and within a year, sales had reached 200. The more powerful and longer-range 747-200 is also available as the -200F freighter, with an upward-hinging nose. The 747SP (Special Performance) has a fuselage shortened by 48ft and was developed for high-capacity long-range routes. The 747's upper deck was stretched for the 747-300, doubling the deck's passenger capacity. The most advanced version is the 747-400. First flown in 1988, it was the first airliner to introduce winglets to reduce drag, and has increased wingspan, a digital flight deck, new engines and greater range. Boeing is planning a new, larger version, the 747-8, to compete with the Airbus A380. Around 1,000 747s are in airline service worldwide.

Statistics

Boeing 747-400

Engines	**Four Pratt & Whitney PW4056/4062 or four General Electric CF6-80C2B or four Rolls-Royce RB211-524 turbofans**
Power	**57,000–63,000lb thrust**
Span	**64.44m (211ft 5in)**
Length	**70.66m (231ft 10in)**
Height	**19.41m (63ft 8in)**
Max weight	**396,895kg (875,000lb)**
Top speed	**939km/h (583mph)**
Cruising speed	**907km/h (564mph)**
Ceiling	**13,746m (45,100ft)**
Range	**13,491km (7,284 miles)**
Flight deck crew	**Two**
Passengers	**up to 660**
First flown	**9 February 1969 (747-100); 29 April 1988 (747-400)**
Into service	**22 January 1970 (747-100)**

Boeing
757

Twin-turbofan, medium/long-range, narrow-body airliner

Boeing
757

Twin-turbofan, medium/long-range, narrow-body airliner

The Boeing 757 was built as a narrow-body successor to the 727, using the same fuselage cross-section. Development of the twin-turbofan 757 was launched in 1979 at the same time as the wide-body 767, with which it shares a common electronic flight deck. The 757 has a new wing and nose and is powered by fuel-efficient turbofan engines. The most numerous version is the 757-200 which entered service in 1983, with seating for 239 passengers. Seating capacity was increased by 20 per cent when the stretched -300 was introduced in 1999. This version has a 7.11m longer fuselage, which also allows 40 per cent more freight to be carried. In 1987 the Rolls-Royce RB211-powered 757 was approved for transatlantic services. Over 1,000 757s are operated worldwide, two-thirds of them in the USA where American (143), Delta (120) and United Airlines (97) are the largest operators. United Parcel Service has a fleet of 75 purpose-built freighters (757-200PFs) and some ex-airline 757s have also been converted to carry cargo, with the designation 757-200SF (Special Freighter). 757 production ended in 2005 after 1,048 had been built.

Statistics

Boeing 757-200

Engines	Two Rolls-Royce RB211-535E4B or two Pratt & Whitney PW2037/2040 turbofans
Power	40,080–43,070lb thrust
Span	38.05m (124ft 10in)
Length	47.32m (155ft 3in)
Height	13.56m (44ft 6in)
Max weight	115,665kg (255,000lb)
Top speed	914km/h (568mph)
Cruising speed	850km/h (528mph)
Ceiling	12,810m (42,000ft)
Range	6,857km (3,700 miles)
Flight deck crew	Two
Passengers	239
First flown	19 February 1982
Into service	1 January 1983

Boeing
767

Twin-turbofan, medium/long-range, wide-body airliner

Boeing
767

Twin-turbofan, medium/long-range, wide-body airliner

First flown in September 1981 (five months before the 757), the twin-turbofan wide-body Boeing 767 was originally designed with a flight crew of three, but was later approved for two-crew operation. The 767's wing has greater sweep than the 757 for more efficient operation at high altitude. With a similar electronic flight deck and systems to the 757, the initial production 767-200 could seat up to 290 passengers. The extra-fuel capacity of the 767-200ER (Extended Range) version allowed it to be flown on transatlantic services. A choice of four different powerplants has been available to 767 customers. A 6.43m increase in fuselage length for the 767-300 increased passenger capacity to 350, and the longer range -300ER followed. To compete with the Airbus A330-200, Boeing developed the 767-400ER, with a further fuselage extension of 6.4m. This has a re-designed cabin, an advanced flight deck similar to the larger 777, plus extended wingtips to improve performance. Delta Air Lines is the biggest operator of 767s, and over 860 are in service around the world.

Boeing 767-300ER

Engines	Two Pratt & Whitney JT9D (or PW4050 series) or two General Electric CF6-80 or two Rolls-Royce RB211-524G/L/H turbofans
Power	56,000–63,000lb thrust
Span	47.57m (156ft 1in)
Length	54.94m (180ft 3in)
Height	15.85m (52ft 0in)
Max weight	186,880kg (412,000lb)
Top speed	900km/h (559mph)
Cruising speed	850km/h (528mph)
Ceiling	13,136m (43,100ft)
Range	11,400km (7,084 miles)
Flight deck crew	Two
Passengers	351
First flown	26 September 1981 (-200); 30 January 1986 (-300)
Into service	26 September 1982 (-200); September 1986 (-300)

Boeing
777

Twin-turbofan, long-range, wide-body airliner

The Boeing 777 is the largest twin-engined aircraft in the world and is fitted with the most powerful engines available. Boeing developed the 777 to compete with long-range Airbus A330s and A340s on intercontinental routes. Designed and built with computer-aided technology, the wide-body 777 makes extensive use of new lightweight composite materials. Parts for some of the airframe are manufactured by partner firms in Japan and sub-contractors around the world, for final assembly by Boeing in the US. It is the most up-to-date Boeing design, with a fly-by-wire control system and advanced 'glass' flight deck. Its increased wing span and additional fuel capacity allow the 777 to fly higher and faster than its competitors. Produced in several versions (-200/-200ER/-200LR & -300/-300ER), the standard -200 first flew in June 1994. The 777-300, with a 10.13m longer fuselage, followed in October 1997. The range of the 777 makes it popular with long-haul airlines from countries such as China, Japan, South Korea, Malaysia and Singapore. By late 2006, the number of 777s in service and on order totalled 844.

Boeing 777-300

Engines	Two Pratt & Whitney PW4090/4098 or two Rolls-Royce Trent 892 turbofans
Power	90,000–98,000lb thrust
Span	60.93m (199ft 11in)
Length	73.86m (242ft 4in)
Height	18.51m (60ft 9in)
Max weight	263,080kg (580,091lb)
Top speed	930km/h (575mph)
Cruising speed	900km/h (560mph)
Ceiling	13,137m (43,100ft)
Range	10,595km (6,583 miles)
Flight deck crew	Two
Passengers	up to 550
First flown	14 June 1994 (777-200); 16 October 1997 (777-300)
Into service	June 1995 (777-200)

Bombardier/Canadair
CRJ

Twin-turbofan, regional airliner series

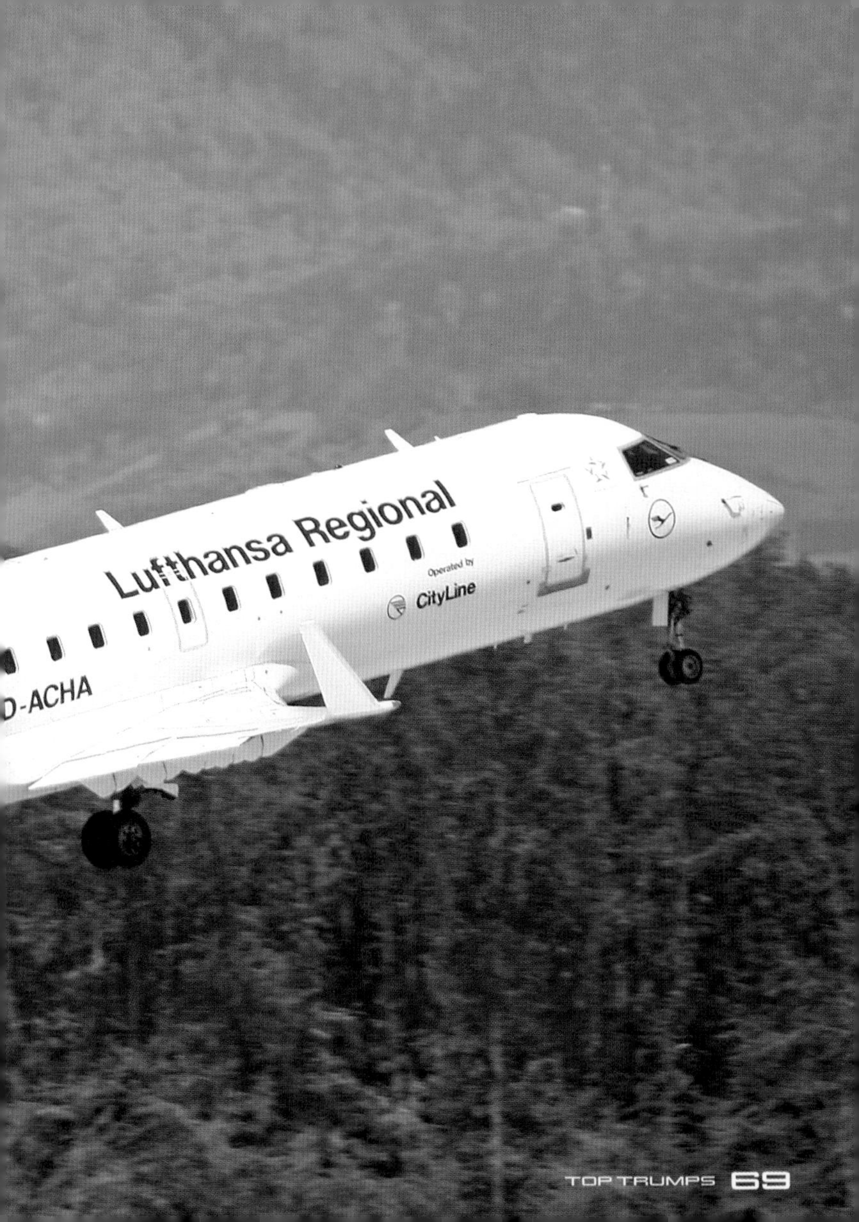
Lufthansa Regional
Operated by
CityLine
D-ACHA

Bombardier/Canadair
CRJ

Twin-turbofan, regional airliner series

Canadian manufacturer Bombardier has achieved great success with the Canadair Regional Jet, a stretched development of the Challenger business jet. It was designed to combine jet speed with lower operating costs. The first CRJ100 carried 50 passengers and had an advanced wing design, electronic flight deck, a new undercarriage and additional fuel capacity. Extended Range and Long Range versions were offered for the CRJ100 and the later -200. The 27-seat Challenger 850 Corporate Shuttle and the reduced-capacity 44-seat CRJ440 are both based on the CRJ200. Production of the 100 and 200 series ended in 2006 after 1,022 had been built. The CRJ700 flew in May 1999 with a fuselage stretch that increased passenger capacity to 70. Bombardier introduced the longer (by 3.8m) CRJ900 in February 2001. It has a stronger airframe and wings and more powerful CF34-8C5 engines. The CRJ705 is based on the CRJ900 and has 75 seats with a 10-seat first class section. Sales of the CRJ700/705 total nearly 300, and orders for CRJ900s have passed 100, 36 of these for Northwest Airlines. Several US regional carriers operate large fleets of mixed-variant CRJs, including SkyWest, Comair, Pinnacle Airlines and Atlantic Southeast Airlines.

Statistics

Bombardier/Canadair CRJ200LR

Engines	Two General Electric CF34-3B1 turbofans
Power	8,729lb thrust
Span	21.21m (69ft 7in)
Length	26.77 (87ft 10in)
Height	6.22m (20ft 5in)
Max weight	24,041kg (53,000lb)
Top speed	860km/h (534mph)
Cruising speed	786km/h (488mph)
Ceiling	12,496m (41,000ft)
Range	3,148km (1,956 miles)
Flight deck crew	Two
Passengers	50
First flown	10 May 1991 (Prototype)
Into service	October 1992 (CRJ-100)

Bombardier/DHC

Dash 8

Twin-turboprop regional airliner

PH-DMR

COMUNITAT
VALENCIANA.com
Comunidad Sede de la 32ª America's Cu

Dash 8-300

Bombardier/DHC
Dash 8

Twin-turboprop regional airliner

Dash 8-Q400

De Havilland Canada developed the twin-engined Dash 8 to seat 30–40 passengers. It retained the high-wing, and T-tail layout of the larger, four-engined Dash 7 and was fitted with large full-span trailing edge flaps. Production began with the Series 100 and the first aircraft was delivered to an airline on 23 October 1984. Engine improvements were introduced for the -200 series, deliveries of which began in April 1995. Since mid-1996, the 'Q' (for 'Quiet') designation has been applied to Dash 8s after the installation of a computer-controlled Noise and Vibration Supression (NVS) system. The Dash 8-300, a 50-seat stretched version, with a 3.43m longer fuselage, flew in May 1987. Bombardier acquired De Havilland Canada from Boeing in 1992, and continued to develop the Dash 8 with a further stretched version, the Q400, first flown in January 1998. The Q400's longer, all-new fuselage with seating increased to 70, retains the distinctive Dash 8 nose shape. Powered by two Pratt & Whitney Canada PW150A turboprops, and equipped with new avionics, the Q400 has five display screens in the cockpit for flight and systems information. Almost 700 Dash 8s were in service at the end of 2006.

Statistics

Bombardier/DHC Dash 8-Q300

Engines	**Two Pratt & Whitney Canada PW123B turboprops**
Power	**2,500shp**
Span	**27.43m (90ft 0in)**
Length	**25.68m (84ft 3in)**
Height	**7.49m (24ft 7in)**
Max weight	**19,505kg (43,000lb)**
Max cruise speed	**532km/h (330mph)**
Ceiling	**7,622m (25,000ft)**
Range	**2,275km (1,413 miles)**
Flight deck crew	**Two**
Passengers	**50**
First flown	**15 May 1987**
Into service	**Late February 1989**

Dash 8-100

British Aerospace
BAe 146/Avro RJ

Four-turbofan regional airliner series

BAe 146-200

British Aerospace
BAe 146/Avro RJ
Four-turbofan regional airliner series

BAe 146-200QC

Hawker Siddeley first proposed a quiet, short-range jet airliner in the early 1970s. It did not go ahead for financial reasons until 1978, when the company became part of British Aerospace. The four-engined BAe 146 first flew in September 1981 and was developed into three versions. The basic 146-100 could seat 70 passengers, which increased to 85 with the introduction of the stretched -200 version in August 1982. A further lengthened version, the 146-300, had seating capacity for up to 128 and first flew in May 1987. A total of 219 BAe 146s was built before production ended in 1993. New-generation versions were then introduced and marketed as the Avro International RJ series. The improved RJ70, RJ85 and RJ100 featured digital flight decks, new engines and modernised cabins, with similar seating layouts to the earlier 146s. The short take-off and landing capabilities and quieter turbofan engines of the 146/RJ series make them ideal for operations into environmentally sensitive and confined airports such as London City. Over 300 146/RJs remain in airline service, mostly on regional services in Europe.

Statistics

BAe 146-300

Engines	Four Textron Lycoming ALF 502R-5 turbofans
Power	6,970lb thrust
Span	26.21m (86ft 0in)
Length	30.99m (101ft 8in)
Height	8.61m (28ft 3in)
Max weight	44,225kg (97,500lb)
Top speed	894km/h (555mph)
Cruising speed	790km/h (491mph)
Ceiling	9,450m (31,000ft)
Range	1,927km (1,197 miles)
Flight deck crew	Two
Passengers	up to 128
First flown	3 September 1981 (prototype)
Into service	May 1983 (146-100)

Avro RJ85

British Aerospace

Jetstream 31

Twin-turboprop, short-range, commuter airliner

Jetstream 31

Twin-turboprop, short-range, commuter airliner

The original design of the Jetstream dates back to the mid-1960s.
Developed by Handley Page, the prototype Jetstream 1 was fitted with
two Turboméca Astazou turboprops and attracted much interest from
commuter airlines and the executive market. However, only 38 had been
delivered when the company ceased trading in 1969. Scottish Aviation
then took on the development of the Jetstream 200 (military versions of
which were supplied to the RAF and Royal Navy) and later the Jetstream
31, after the company became part of British Aerospace. The J31 was
powered by two Garret TPE331 engines and first flew in March 1980. The
first production aircraft flew two years later. The Jetstream's performance
was improved with the introduction of the Super 31 (Jetstream 32), which
featured up-rated engines and higher weights. The longer-range J32EP
(Enhanced Performance) is fitted with a pannier under the fuselage
to increase the payload and can operate in 'hot and high' conditions.
Production of the J31 totalled 381, of which 161 were Super J31s. Over 150
remain in service worldwide.

Statistics

BAe Jetstream 31

Engines	Two Garret TPE331-10 turboprops
Power	940shp
Span	15.85m (52ft 0in)
Length	14.37m (47ft 2in)
Height	5.37m (17ft 6in)
Max weight	6,950kg (15,322lb)
Top speed	482km/h (300 mph)
Cruising speed	426km/h (265 mph)
Ceiling	7,620m (25,000ft)
Range	1185km (640 miles)
Flight deck crew	Two
Passengers	18
First flown	18 August 1967 (Jetstream 1); 18 March 1980 (J31)
Into service	June 1982 (J31)

British Aerospace

Jetstream 41

Short-range, twin-turboprop regional airliner

British Aerospace

Jetstream 41

Short-range, twin-turboprop regional airliner

Designed to compete with regional turboprop airliners such as the
Embraer Brasilia, Dornier 328 and Saab 340, the Jetstream 41 is an
updated stretched version of the earlier J31, that can seat up to 29
passengers. The Jetstream 41's fuselage is 4.88m longer overall than
the J31 and its wingspan is increased by 2.44m. The more powerful
AlliedSignal TPE331 turboprops, fitted with new technology five-bladed
propellers, are mounted higher on the wings to give greater ground
clearance. This made it possible to position the wing lower on the
fuselage in order to maintain an unobstructed interior cabin aisle, and
the flatter tail assembly gives the J41 a much lower appearance on the
ground than the J31. A redesigned cockpit features modern digital 'glass'
display screens. The Jetstream 41 was first flown in 1991, and production
was terminated in 1998 after a total of 100 had been built. The J41's range
and payload were improved during production with the introduction of
up-rated engines. Over half remain in service, the only European operator
being the UK's Eastern Airways with a fleet of 25 J41s, together with a
small number of J31/32s.

Statistics

BAe Jetstream 41

Engines	**Two AlliedSignal TPE331-14HR/GR turboprops**
Power	**1,650shp**
Span	**18.29m (60ft 0in)**
Length	**19.25m (63ft 2in)**
Height	**5.74m (18ft 10in)**
Max weight	**10,895kg (24,000lb)**
Top speed	**547km/h (340mph)**
Cruising speed	**482km/h (300mph)**
Ceiling	**7,925m (26,000ft)**
Range	**1,433km (890 miles)**
Flight deck crew	**Two**
Passengers	**29**
First flown	**25 September 1991**
Into service	**25 November 1992**

Britten-Norman
Islander

Twin piston or turboprop, short-range, utility transport series

BN-2B

Britten-Norman

Islander

Twin piston or turboprop, short-range, utility transport series

G-TWOB

BN-2A

The Britten-Norman Islander is the most successful British commercial aircraft. John Britten and Desmond Norman first produced this rugged twin-engined light transport aircraft in the mid-1960s. Low operating costs and ease of maintenance have helped the Islander's popularity, sales of which had reached 1,250 in 2006. First flown in 1965, the Islander is still in production today, although aircraft are assembled in Romania before completion in the UK. The Islander's box-like cabin has no central aisle, with passengers getting to their seats via three doors on either side of the fuselage. The early piston-engined BN-2A version was improved with engine upgrades and increased fuel capacity. After Pilatus acquired B-N in 1979, production of the BN-2B began. This version had higher weights, a redesigned cabin and other internal improvements. The BN-2T turbine-engined Islander first flew in August 1980. BN-2T-4S versions are used for surveillance by several UK police forces. In 1970 B-N produced the three-engined BN-2A Mk III Trislander, doubling the Islander's passenger capacity. The additional engine was mounted on the tail fin. Trislander production totalled 73 aircraft.

Statistics

Britten-Norman BN-2B Islander

Engines	**Two Textron Lycoming IO-540 piston engines**
Power	**300hp**
Span	**14.94m (49ft 0in)**
Length	**10.86 (35ft 8in)**
Height	**4.18m (13ft 9in)**
Max weight	**2,993kg (6,600lb)**
Top speed	**280km/h (174mph)**
Cruising speed	**264km/h (164mph)**
Ceiling	**5,242m (17,200ft)**
Range	**1,136km (706 miles)**
Flight deck crew	**One/two**
Passengers	**8/9**
First flown	**13 June 1965 (Prototype)**
Into service	**August 1967 (BN-2)**

BN-2A

BN-2A MkIII Trislander

CASA
212

Twin-turboprop, short-range transport

EC-INX

M.A.
SECRETARIA GENERA

CASA
212

Twin-turboprop, short-range transport

First flown in 1971, the CASA 212 Aviocar was developed as a replacement for the Spanish Air Force's ageing transport fleet, but with appeal to civil operators. The high-mounted wings gave excellent landing and take-off performance, and its rugged construction allowed operations in tough conditions. The first commercial C-212C was delivered in 1975 and production continued until 1978, when it was replaced on the line by the more powerful C-212-200. This increase in power allowed higher operating weights. The stretched C-212-300 followed, with engine improvements and the addition of winglets to improve aerodynamic efficiency. The latest version, the C-212-400, first flew in 1997. This version is fitted with an advanced 'glass' cockpit and is powered by AlliedSignal TPE331-12JR turboprops, giving better 'hot and high' performance. Up to 26 passengers can be carried in the square cross-section cabin. The C-212 is popular with regional airlines in Third World countries due to its performance, and substantial sales of military variants have been achieved. Sales of the 212 have reached around 450, about 170 of these for commercial operators. IPTN produce the C-212 under licence in Indonesia, where it is marketed as the Indonesian Aerospace 212.

CASA 212-300

Engines	Two Garret AiResearch (now AlliedSignal) TPE331-10R turboprops
Power	900shp
Span	20.28m (66ft 7in)
Length	16.15m (53ft 0in)
Height	6.60m (21ft 8in)
Max weight	7,000kg (16,925lb)
Top speed	370km/h (231mph)
Cruising speed	300km/h (186mph)
Ceiling	7,925m (26,000ft)
Range	1,435km (892 miles)
Flight deck crew	Two
Passengers	26
First flown	26 March 1971 (prototype)
Into service	July 1975 (C-212C)

De Havilland Canada
DHC-6 Twin Otter

Twin-turboprop, short-range commuter airliner

De Havilland Canada
DHC-6 Twin Otter
Twin-turboprop, short-range commuter airliner

The Twin Otter remains the most successful commercial aircraft produced in Canada. It was designed as a small regional airliner with seating for up to 20 passengers. Experience gained with its earlier single-engined DHC-2 Beaver and DHC-3 Otter designs enabled DHC to give the Twin Otter an impressive STOL (Short Take-Off and Landing) performance. A total of 115 Series 100s was built before production switched to the Series 200, that had a longer nose giving greater baggage capacity. The final Series 300 had uprated engines that increased the maximum take-off weight. Sales of 614 DHC-6-300s made this the most popular version. Twin Otters were ideal for commuter and third-level airline use, and during the 1970s six specially-modified DHC-6s evaluated the operation of commuter aircraft from 'STOLports' set up close to major city centres. The performance of these aircraft, operated by AirTransit, was helped by the addition of wing spoilers. A pair of ski-equipped Twin Otters are used by the British Antarctic Expedition. A total of 844 had been built when production ended in 1988, and of these about 350 remain in commercial service.

Statistics

DHC-6-300 Twin Otter

Engines	Two Pratt & Whitney Canada PT6A-27 turboprops
Power	620shp
Span	19.81m (65ft 0in)
Length	15.77m (51ft 9in)
Height	5.94m (19ft 6in)
Max weight	5,670kg (12,500lb)
Top speed	338km/h (210mph)
Cruising speed	297km/h (185mph)
Ceiling	8,140m (26,700ft)
Range	1,297km (806 miles)
Flight deck crew	Two
Passengers	20
First flown	20 May 1965 (prototype)
Into service	July 1966 (DHC-6-100)

Dornier
328

Twin-turboprop regional airliner

G-CJAC

328 CORPORATE

Dornier 328

Dornier
328

Twin-turboprop regional airliner

Dornier 328

The success of its 228 15-seat regional turboprop in the early 1980s encouraged Dornier to develop a larger airliner with twice the capacity. First flown in 1991, the Dornier 328 has a very clean wing design that gives high speed climb and cruise performance. Composite materials are used in the fuselage and tail construction to save weight. Three-abreast seating makes the 328 even roomier than Boeing's 727 and 737 jets. Several partner firms (Daewoo, Aermacchi, Westland and Israel Aircraft Industries) contributed to the 328's construction, accounting for 40% of the airframe. In mid-1996 Fairchild Aerospace acquired 80% of Dornier and within a year had launched the 328JET to create a new 30-seat regional jet. The prototype (a converted 328 turboprop) flew on 20 January 1998. The new 32-seat aircraft was fitted with Pratt & Whitney Canada PW306 turbofans and an auxiliary power unit (APU) as standard. In 2002, Fairchild Dornier collapsed and AvCraft Aerospace took on the rights to 328/328JET production. After this company also failed, a German company was set up in 2006 to provide worldwide 328/328JET support. A total of 107 328s and 109 328JETs was built.

Dornier 328-110

Engines	Two Pratt & Whitney Canada PW119B turboprops
Power	2,180shp
Span	20.98m (68ft 10in)
Length	21.22 (69ft 8in)
Height	7.24m (23ft 9in)
Max weight	13,990kg (30,842lb)
Top speed	640km/h (398mph)
Cruising speed	620km/h (385mph)
Ceiling	9,450m (31,000ft)
Range	1,665km (900 miles)
Flight deck crew	Two
Passengers	30
First flown	6 December 1991 (328-100)
Into service	October 1993 (328-100)

Dornier 328 JET

Dornier 328 JET

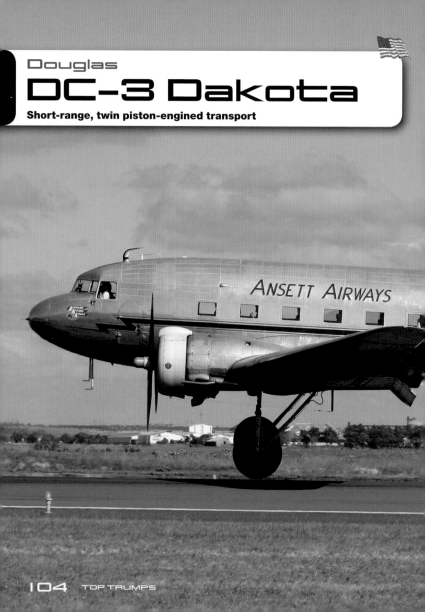

Douglas
DC-3 Dakota
Short-range, twin piston-engined transport

Douglas
DC-3 Dakota

Short-range, twin piston-engined transport

Known as 'the workhorse of the skies', the DC-3 Dakota has enjoyed commercial success ever since its first flight in 1935. The DC-3 began life as the Douglas Sleeper Transport (DST), for use on US transcontinental routes. Its clean design and economic operation quickly made it a popular choice for US airlines. Although World War II halted commercial production, the DC-3 was developed as the C-47 military transport and over 10,000 were built. Post-war, large numbers of these were sold to civil operators, and they became the standard airliner around the world. The introduction of larger and more powerful airliners – and jets from the mid-1950s – relegated the DC-3 to less important routes. Its rugged and reliable performance made the DC-3 ideal for operations using unprepared airstrips, favouring use by airlines in countries in South America, Africa and Asia. Remaining DC-3s are mainly used as freighters. The type was built under licence in Japan and Russia, and the many military versions included ski-equipped R4Ds, one of which became the first aircraft to land at the South Pole in October 1956.

Douglas C-47A

Engines	Two Pratt & Whitney R-1830 Twin Wasp or two Wright Cyclone SGR-1820 radial piston engines
Power	1,200hp
Span	29.11m (95ft 6in)
Length	19.43m (63ft 9in)
Height	5.18m (17ft 0in)
Max weight	12,700kg (28,000lb)
Top speed	370km/h (230mph)
Cruising speed	266km/h (165mph)
Ceiling	7,315m (24,000ft)
Range	2,575km (1,600 miles)
Flight deck crew	Two
Passengers	32
First flown	17 December 1935 (DST)
Into service	25 June 1936 (DST)

Douglas
DC-4 Skymaster

Four piston-engined, medium/long-range transport series

DC-4

Douglas
DC-4 Skymaster
Four piston-engined, medium/long-range transport series

DC-6B

The successful Douglas family of 'propliners' continued with the four-engined DC-4. Although development had begun in 1938, the attack on Pearl Harbor in 1941 and subsequent US involvement in WWII meant that the first aircraft emerged as the military C-54 Skymaster transport in February 1942. Over 1,000 were built, and post-war many were converted to carry passengers and sold to airlines. The longer-range DC-6 used the same wing as the DC-4 but with a larger, pressurised fuselage. The main DC-6B version was bought by major airlines worldwide and together with the Lockheed Constellation, it dominated the airliner market in the 1950s. To match Lockheed's Super Constellation, Douglas developed the DC-7, which had a stretched fuselage and could seat up to 95 passengers. On 25 April 1955, Pan Am operated the first non-stop New York–London transatlantic service with a DC-7B. The final DC-7C Seven Seas had greater range, and flew the first 'over-the-pole' service between Europe and the Far East. Many DC-4s, -6s and -7s have ended up converted as cargo carriers and water-bombers.

Douglas DC-6B

Engines	Four Pratt & Whitney Double Wasp R-2800-CB17 radial piston engines
Power	2,500hp
Span	35.81m (117ft 6in)
Length	32.18m (105ft 7in)
Height	8.66m (28ft 5in)
Max weight	48,534kg (107,000lb)
Top speed	570km/h (354mph)
Cruising speed	507km/h (315mph)
Ceiling	8,840m (29,000ft)
Range	4,835km (3,005 miles)
Flight deck crew	Three or four
Passengers	102
First flown	9 July 1946 (DC-6)
Into service	27 April 1947 (DC-6)

DC-4

DC-6B

Douglas
DC-8

Four-turbofan, long-range, narrow-body airliner series

Douglas
DC-8

Four-turbofan, long-range, narrow-body airliner series

DC-8-73

The new jet age saw Boeing take the lead with its 707. Douglas therefore proposed the DC-8, of similar appearance with swept wings and four underwing turbojets. First flown in May 1958, the DC-8-10 was produced for US domestic use with United and Delta Air Lines. The Series 20 followed with uprated JT4A turbojets for 'hot and high' operations. Intercontinental range was achieved with the DC-8-30 Series, having increased fuel and payload. Rolls-Royce Conway bypass engines were fitted to the Series 40, and the DC-8-50 introduced new Pratt & Whitney JT3D turbofans with passenger seating increased to 189. To attract new customers, from 1966 Douglas produced the stretched DC-8 'Super' Series. The last of these, the Super 63, combined the Super 61's 11.18m fuselage stretch with the Super 62's longer wings, for transatlantic operation. All-cargo and convertible passenger/freight versions of the DC-8 were already popular before the re-engining of the Supers with more powerful CFM56 turbofans began in the early 1980s to produce the DC-8-71,-72 and -73 series. Production of the DC-8 ended in 1972 after a total of 556 had been built. A small number remain in service with cargo operators.

Douglas DC-8-61

Engines	Two Pratt & Whitney JT3D-3 turbofans
Power	18,000lb thrust
Span	43.41m (142ft 5in)
Length	57.10m (187ft 4in)
Height	13.11m (43ft 0in)
Max weight	147,415kg (325,000lb)
Top speed	935km/h (581mph)
Cruising speed	851km/h (529mph)
Ceiling	10,668m (35,000ft)
Range	6,035km (3,750 miles)
Flight deck crew	Three
Passengers	259
First flown	30 May 1958 (Prototype)
Into service	18 September 1959 (DC-8-10)

DC-8-73

DC-8-55

mbraer
EMB-120 Brasilia
n-turboprop, regional airliner

EMB-120 Brasilia

Twin-turboprop, regional airliner

The EMB-120 was designed as a 30-seat pressurised airliner by Brazilian manufacturer Embraer in the early 1980s. It was a progression from the successful 15–18 seat EMB-110 Bandeirante and smaller EMB-121 Xingu. First flown in July 1983, the Brasilia had a longer fuselage, T-tail configuration (like the Xingu) and was powered by Pratt & Whitney Canada PW115 turboprops. A number of versions have been built with more powerful PW118 engines, including the EMB-120RT (Reduced Take-off weight), the Extended Range EMB-120ER, EMB-120 Cargo freighter, and EMB-120 Combi (mixed passenger/cargo) and Quick-Change (QC) models. All these versions were also available with uprated PW118A engines for 'hot and high' operation. The Brasilia remains in production with the EMB-120ER Advanced, which entered airline service in 1993. It has improvements to the design of the wings, flight deck and passenger cabin. The fuselage of the Brasilia was later adapted as the basis for Embraer's EMB-145 regional jet. Over 350 EMB-120s have been delivered to airlines. SkyWest Airlines in the USA is the largest operator with a fleet of 54 -120ERs and 14 -120RTs.

Embraer EMB-120 Brasilia Advanced

Engines	Two Pratt & Whitney PW118B turboprops
Power	1,800shp
Span	19.78m (64ft 11in)
Length	20.00m (65ft 7in)
Height	6.35m (20ft 10in)
Max weight	11,990kg (26,433lb)
Top speed	582km/h (362mph)
Cruising speed	555km/h (345mph)
Ceiling	9,753m (32,000ft)
Range	1,481km (920 miles)
Flight deck crew	Two
Passengers	30
First flown	27 July 1983 (prototype)
Into service	October 1985 (EMB-120)

Embraer
ERJ-145

Twin-turbofan, regional airliner series

ERJ-145

Twin-turbofan, regional airliner series

ERJ-145

With worldwide sales of the narrow-body ERJ-135/140/145 series approaching 1,000, Embraer has become one of the leading manufacturers of regional jets. The ERJ-145, which was first flown (as the EMB-145) on 11 August 1995, was based on the company's earlier Brasilia, with new wings, a T-tail and lengthened fuselage. It is powered by two rear fuselage-mounted Rolls-Royce AE 3007A turbofans. Passenger capacity of the ERJ-145 is 50, whilst the shorter-fuselage ERJ-135 seats 37. This version flew in July 1998, followed by the 44-seat ERJ-140 three years later. Long Range (LR) and Extended Range (ER) versions were produced, plus an ERJ-145XR Extra-long Range variant with winglets, an additional ventral (underneath) fuel tank and more powerful engines. The success of Embraer's bigger 'E-Jet' family of regional airliners slowed down orders for the ERJ series, and ERJ-145 production is now in China, where Harbin is assembling 50 aircraft for Hainan Airlines. First delivery of the ERJ-145 was to Express Jet Airlines, now the largest operator with 244 (plus 30 ERJ-135s). The ERJ-145 family of aircraft are in service today with 87 different airlines around the world.

Statistics

Embraer ERJ-145LR

Engines	**Two Rolls-Royce AE 3007A turbofans**
Power	**7,420lb thrust**
Span	**20.04m (65ft 9in)**
Length	**29.87m (98ft 0in)**
Height	**6.75m (22ft 2in)**
Max weight	**20,600kg (45,414lb)**
Top speed	**834km/h (518mph)**
Cruising speed	**797km/h (495mph)**
Ceiling	**11,278m (37,000ft)**
Range	**2,775km (1,724 miles)**
Flight deck crew	**Two**
Passengers	**50**
First flown	**11 August 1995 (prototype)**
Into service	**Early 1997 (ERJ-145)**

Embraer
E170

Twin-turbofan, medium-range regional airliner series

Embraer
E170

Twin-turbofan, medium-range regional airliner series

Using the success of its ERJ series, Embraer has developed a new 'family' of larger commercial airliners, known as E-Jets. Launched in 1999, the range consists of four basic models – the 70-seat 170, 78-seat 175, 98-seat 190 and the 108-seat 195. The E170/175 variants are designed to compete with regional jets such as the Bombardier CRJ-900 and replace older types like the BAe 146. The larger E190 and E195 are comparable to the Boeing 737-600 and Airbus A318/319. The first of six development aircraft for the E170 programme flew in February 2002, and the stretched E175 followed in June 2003. The E190 and E195 variants both flew in 2004. All are powered by fully-interchangeable General Electric CF34 engines, and use state-of-the-art technology with fly-by-wire flight controls and an electronic flight deck. The E175 has a fuselage stretch 1.77m longer than the E170, and the E190 is extended by a further 4.56m. The longest E-Jet is the E195, with a fuselage 8.75m longer than the E170. The fuselage allows four-abreast seating with a central aisle. Over 540 E-Jets had been ordered by late 2006, mostly E-190s.

Statistics

Embraer 170LR

Engines	Two General Electric CF34-8E turbofans
Power	14,200lb thrust
Span	26.00m (85ft 4in)
Length	29.90m (98ft 1in)
Height	9.85m (32ft 4in)
Max weight	48,500kg (106,922lb)
Top speed	890km/h (553mph)
Cruising speed	870km/h (540mph)
Ceiling	12,500m (41,000ft)
Range	3,889km (2,416 miles)
Flight deck crew	Two
Passengers	70
First flown	19 February 2002
Into service	March 2004

Fairchild/Swearingen

Metro

Twin-turboprop, regional airliner

N27244

Fairchild/Swearingen
Metro
Twin-turboprop, regional airliner

First flown in August 1969, the Metro was a longer, pressurised development of Swearingen's Merlin business turboprop. The 19-seat Metro became one of the most popular commuter aircraft in its class. Swearingen was acquired by the Fairchild Aircraft Corporation in 1971, and Air Wisconsin became the first airline operator of the Metro in 1972. The Metro has a distinctive long narrow fuselage with large square cabin windows and an extended nose. The pair of TPE331 turboprops are mounted on short straight wings. Maximum weights of both the Metro I and II were limited by FAA regulations, but the later Metro III was certified up to 14,000lb and featured a 3.05m increase in wing span, winglets and uprated engines with four-bladed propellers. Further increases in systems, power and weight, achieved as a result of developing the military C-26 version for the US services, resulted in the Metro 23. Greater baggage capacity was a feature of the Metro 23EF, which had a bulged lower fuselage. The Expediter freight model was fitted with a large rear door and a reinforced floor. A total of 619 Metros had been built when production ended in 2001.

Fairchild Metro III

Engines	Two Garret TPE331-11U-612G turboprops
Power	1,100shp
Span	17.37m (57ft 0in)
Length	18.09m (59ft 4in)
Height	5.08m (16ft 8in)
Max weight	7,257kg (16,000lb)
Top speed	576km/h (358mph)
Cruising speed	515km/h (320mph)
Ceiling	7,620m (25,000ft)
Range	2,131km (1,324 miles)
Flight deck crew	Two
Passengers	19
First flown	26 August 1969 (prototype)
Into service	1972 (Metro I)

Fokker
F.27 Friendship
Twin-turboprop regional airliner series

N278MA

F-27-200

Fokker
F.27 Friendship

Twin-turboprop regional airliner series

Fokker 50

Dutch manufacturer Fokker produced the F.27 Friendship for 30 years up to 1985, making it the most successful Western turboprop airliner ever produced. Intended as a DC-3 replacement, the high-wing pressurised F.27 was powered by two Rolls-Royce Darts. The initial F.27 Mk 100 had seating for 32, and later versions included the Mk 200, Mk 400 Combi (passenger/cargo) and the stretched 52-seat Mk 500. In 1956, licence production of the F-27 by Fairchild began, the first US-built aircraft flying in April 1958. Fairchild also produced the stretched FH-227, which had a 1.83m increase over the standard F.27. Popular around the world, many civil and military versions remain in service, including cargo variants. Fokker production, including military Troopships and Maritime Patrol Aircraft, totalled 581. Fairchild built 128 F-27s and 78 FH-227s. The Friendship's successor, the faster Fokker 50, first flew in 1985. Although very similar in appearance, it had new generation Pratt & Whitney Canada PW125B engines with six-blade propellers, new avionics and 'glass' flight deck, plus increased range. Smaller, squarer windows replaced the F.27's distinctive oval-shaped windows. A total of 205 Fokker 50s had been built when Fokker ran into financial trouble in 1996.

Fokker F.27 Mk 500 Friendship

Engines	**Two Rolls-Royce Dart Mk 536 turboprops**
Power	**2,140shp**
Span	**29.00m (95ft 2in)**
Length	**23.06m (82ft 3in)**
Height	**8.71m (28ft 7in)**
Max weight	**20,410kg (44,996lb)**
Top speed	**473km/h (294mph)**
Cruising speed	**435km/h (270mph)**
Ceiling	**8,992m (29,500ft)**
Range	**1,468km (912 miles)**
Flight deck crew	**Two**
Passengers	**52**
First flown	**24 November 1955 (prototype)**
Into service	**September 1958 (Fairchild FH-227)**

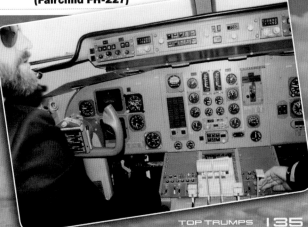

F-27

Fokker
F.28 Fellowship
Twin-turbofan, short-range, regional airliner series

Fokker 100

F.28 Fellowship

Twin-turbofan, short-range, regional airliner series

Fokker 70

Fokker had entered the jet airliner market in 1967, when it flew the prototype 55-seat F.28 Fellowship twin-engined regional airliner. It remained in production until 1987, when the last of 241 F.28s was built. Announced at the same time as the Fokker 50 turboprop, the Fokker 100 was an updated, longer-fuselage development of the F.28 design. To meet new European aircraft noise regulations, the 100 was fitted with economical and quieter Rolls-Royce Tay turbofans. It also had a revised wing, flight deck and cabin. The standard Fokker 100 could seat 100 passengers. First flown in November 1986, it was joined on the production line in the 1990s by the shorter, modified Fokker 70, designed to replace older F.28s. Flown in July 1994, the first Fokker 70 delivery was made in October the same year. Although the Fokker 100 outsold the F.28, sales of the Fokker 70 were disappointing. After the company collapsed, the production line closed in 1997, with 283 Fokker 100s and 48 Fokker 70s delivered. Most remain in service today, with KLM Cityhopper (22 Fokker 70s and 18 Fokker 100s) the main operator.

Statistics

Fokker 100

Engines	Two Rolls-Royce Tay 650 turbofans
Power	15,100lb thrust
Span	28.08m (92ft 2in)
Length	35.53m (116ft 7in)
Height	8.51m (27ft 11in)
Max weight	45,810kg (101,000lb)
Top speed	845km/h (525mph)
Cruising speed	755km/h (469mph)
Ceiling	11,300m (37,000ft)
Range	3,167km (1,967 miles)
Flight deck crew	Two
Passengers	107
First flown	30 November 1986
Into service	February 1988

Fokker 70

Fokker 100

RA-96101

Il-96

Ilyushin
Il-86

Four turbofan, medium/long-range wide-body airliner series

The Ilyushin Il-86 was the first wide-body airliner produced in the Soviet Union. The prototype flew in December 1976 after a long development period. Production aircraft did not enter service until four years later. The Il-86 had a conventional layout, with four podded engines mounted under swept wings. An unusual feature was the use of self-contained steps that allowed passengers to board via the lower fuselage before climbing internal stairs to the main cabin. Production ended in 1994 after 103 had been built, all of which were delivered to Russian airlines. In the mid 1980s, Ilyushin began developing a new widebody airliner that would overcome the Il-86's shortcomings. It emerged as the Il-96 and was first flown in September 1988, entering service with the Russian state airline Aeroflot in 1993. The Il-96 is a new-generation airliner, with a shorter fuselage and new wing with winglets, and the ability to fly further than the Il-86. It also has a fly-by-wire flight control system and a modern flight deck. By late 2006, orders for the Il-96-300 totalled 19, with production due to switch to the larger Il-96-400. This version will have more powerful 38,500lb thrust PS-90A1 engines and a range of 5,000km.

Statistics

Ilyushin Il-96-300

Engines	Four Aviadvigatel PS-90A turbofans
Power	35,250lb thrust
Span	60.11m (197ft 3in)
Length	55.35m (181ft 7in)
Height	17.55m (57ft 7in)
Max weight	216,000kg (476,200lb)
Top speed	900km/h (560mph)
Cruising speed	850km/h (528mph)
Ceiling	12,192m (40,000ft)
Range	7,500km (4,660 miles)
Flight deck crew	Three
Passengers	up to 300
First flown	28 September 1988
Into service	1993

Il-96

Il-86

Let
L-410 Turbolet

Twin-turboprop regional airliner

OK-ODF

L-410 Turbolet

Twin-turboprop regional airliner

The Czech-built L-410 was produced as a robust commuter transport
for the Russian and Soviet-influenced eastern European markets.
The compact 19-seater is comparable to the DHC-6 Twin Otter, and
was designed for operation from unprepared airstrips. Powered by
Pratt & Whitney Canada PT-6A engines, the prototype L-410 first flew
in 1969. Walter (Motorlet) M601A turboprops were introduced in 1973
for production L-410Ms. The Turbolet has a high-wing layout, and the
fuselage features double upward-opening doors on the left side. Stub
fairings on the lower fuselage permit the retraction of the mainwheels.
Initial production L-410As were replaced by the slightly longer fuselage
L-410UVP in 1979, followed by the L-410UVP-E with revised cabin layout.
Approximately 1,100 L-410s have been built, many of which are now in
service with eastern European regional airlines. Substantial numbers of
L-410s also operate in Africa and South America, where the aircraft is
ideally suited to the environment. A specially-modified photo-survey
version known as the L-410AF had a larger and wider glazed nose that
housed a vertically-mounted camera.

Let L-410UVP-E

Engines	Two Motorlet M601E turboprops
Power	750shp
Span	19.98m (65ft 7in)
Length	14.43m (47ft 4in)
Height	5.83m (19ft 2in)
Max weight	6,600kg (14,550lb)
Top speed	388km/h (241mph)
Cruising speed	365km/h (227mph)
Ceiling	7,406m (24,300ft)
Range	560km (348 miles)
Flight deck crew	Two
Passengers	19
First flown	16 April 1969 (XL-410 prototype)
Into service	1971 (L-410A)

Lockheed
TriStar

Medium/long-range, tri-turbofan, wide-body airliner

Lockheed
TriStar

Medium/long-range, tri-turbofan, wide-body airliner

The TriStar was the last airliner produced by Lockheed. It was developed to meet a mid-1960s American Airlines requirement for a large-capacity medium-range airliner. Similar in layout to its competitor, the McDonnell Douglas DC-10 (which flew first, in August 1970), the TriStar differed by having its third engine built into the rear fuselage, whereas the DC-10's rear engine was mounted on the tail. First flight of the L-1011 took place on 16 November 1970, and although the DC-10 was eventually chosen by American Airlines, orders from Eastern and TWA enabled the TriStar to go into production. Early problems with the Rolls-Royce RB211 engine arose when the engine manufacturer went bankrupt in February 1971, and DC-10 sales increased as a result. The engine problems were eventually overcome, and Lockheed was able to begin deliveries in 1972. Main versions were the -100 (more fuel/higher weight), -200 (uprated engines) and the -500, a long-range smaller capacity variant based on the -200 with a 4.11m reduction in fuselage length. Major airlines that ordered TriStars included Air Canada, British Airways, Delta, Pan Am, Saudia and Cathay Pacific. TriStar production totalled 250.

Statistics

Lockheed L-1011-200 TriStar

Engines	**Three Rolls-Royce RB211-524 turbofans**
Power	**48,000lb thrust**
Span	**47.34m (155ft 4in)**
Length	**54.17m (177ft 8in)**
Height	**16.87m (55ft 4in)**
Max weight	**211,375kg (466,000lb)**
Top speed	**973km/h (605mph)**
Cruising speed	**890km/h (553mph)**
Ceiling	**13,259m (43,500ft)**
Range	**6,820km (4,238 miles)**
Flight deck crew	**Three**
Passengers	**up to 400**
First flown	**16 November 1970 (Prototype)**
Into service	**26 April 1972 (-100)**

McDonnell Douglas
DC-9

Twin-turbofan, short-range, narrow-body airliner

McDonnell Douglas
DC-9

Twin-turbofan, short-range, narrow-body airliner

The DC-9 was the most successful airliner produced by the Douglas Aircraft Company. Similar in appearance to the British BAC-111 that flew in August 1963, the twin-jet DC-9 adopted the same layout with a T-tail, swept wings and rear-mounted engines. It went on to achieve worldwide sales, and Douglas offered it in a number of versions that matched the requirements of particular airlines. The short fuselage Series 10 was increased in length by 4.6m to create the Series 30, which was the most numerous version, with sales reaching almost 600 before production ended in 1982. Further increases in length produced the Series 40 and Series 50. Seating capacity increased to 139 from the original 90 of the DC-9-10. Douglas was taken over by McDonnell in 1967, and later developments of the DC-9 were produced as the MD-80 series. Over 400 DC-9s are still in operation, the majority in North and South America. Northwest Airlines has a fleet of over 100 DC-9-30s. Overall production totalled 976.

Statistics

McDonnell Douglas DC-9-30

Engines	Two Pratt & Whitney JT8D-9 (or JT8D-11/17s) turbofans
Power	16,000 lb thrust (JT8D-17s)
Span	28.47m (93ft 5in)
Length	36.37m (119ft 4in)
Height	8.38m (27ft 6in)
Max weight	54,885kg (121,000lb)
Top speed	907km/h (564mph)
Cruising speed	798km/h (496mph)
Ceiling	10,975m (36,000ft)
Range	3095km (1,670 miles) (with max payload)
Flight deck crew	Two
Passengers	up to 115
First flown	25 February 1965 (DC-9 prototype)
Into service	8 December 1965 (DC-9-10)

McDonnell Douglas
MD-80

Twin-turbofan, short/medium-range airliner series

McDonnell Douglas
MD-80
Twin-turbofan, short/medium-range airliner series

In the early 1980s the availability of powerful new turbofans enabled McDonnell Douglas to offer an improved, longer fuselage version of the DC-9, known as the DC-9 Super 80. It became the MD-80 series in 1983 with the first version, Swissair's MD-81, followed by the MD-82 with improved JT8D-217 engines, and the longer-range MD-83. Flown in December 1986, the short-fuselage MD-87 was similar to the DC-9-30 but was the first of the MD-80 series to feature an Electronic Flight Information Systems (EFIS) 'glass' flight deck. The last of the series, the MD-88, had a re-designed cabin and uprated engines. In 1993 McDonnell Douglas flew the MD-90, the largest aircraft in the DC-9 'family'. The MD-90's fuel-efficient IAE V2500 turbofans are the largest, heaviest and most powerful engines ever to be rear-mounted on an airliner. A forward fuselage 'plug' of 1.4m was added that also allowed an extra ten passengers to be carried. After Boeing merged with McDonnell Douglas, the MD-80/90 series was discontinued in 2000. Boeing developed the MD-95 proposal as the 100-seat Boeing 717 short-range regional airliner. Production of the MD-80/90 series totalled 1,307 and over 1,200 of these remain in airline service.

McDonnell Douglas MD-83

Engines	**Two Pratt & Whitney JT8D-219 turbofans**
Power	**21,690lb thrust**
Span	**32.87m (107ft 10in)**
Length	**45.1m (147ft 10in)**
Height	**9.02m (29ft 8in)**
Max weight	**72,576kg (160,000lb)**
Top speed	**925km/h (575mph)**
Cruising speed	**813km/h (505mph)**
Ceiling	**11,277m (37,000ft)**
Range	**4,635km (2,880 miles)**
Flight deck crew	**Two**
Passengers	**up to 168**
First flown	**17 December 1984**
Into service	**July 1985**

McDonnell Douglas
DC-10

Medium/long-range, tri-turbofan, wide-body airliner

McDonnell Douglas
DC-10

Medium/long-range, tri-turbofan, wide-body airliner

The tri-jet wide-body DC-10 was launched as a direct competitor to Lockheed's similar TriStar. First flown in August 1970, the DC-10-10 version entered service with American Airlines and United Airlines on domestic routes in the USA. Transatlantic flights commenced in December 1972 when Swissair put the longer-range DC-10-30 into service. Other versions were the -15 (for 'hot and high' operations), -30CF (passenger/cargo convertible) and the all-cargo -30F. The DC-10 gained publicity when Laker Airways began its no-reservation 'Skytrain' service from London to New York in 1977. However, major accidents involving DC-10s in 1974 and 1979, together with the introduction of more economical twin-jet wide-body airliners, had a bad effect on sales. Production ended in 1989 after 386 civil DC-10s had been built, and the DC-10 was re-launched as the MD-11. The air freight company Federal Express (FedEx) started a programme in 1996 to convert ex-airline DC-10-10s into cargo aircraft. They are fitted with an MD-11-type two-crew Advanced Common Flightdeck (ACF). In 2006, a converted DC-10 'Super Tanker', capable of dropping up to 45,600 litres from an under-fuselage tank, was approved for use as an aerial firefighter.

McDonnell Douglas DC-10-30ER

Engines	**Three General Electric CF6-50C turbofans**
Power	**53,200lb thrust**
Span	**50.39m (165ft 4in)**
Length	**55.35m (181ft 7in)**
Height	**17.7m (58ft 1in)**
Max weight	**263,085kg (580,000lb)**
Top speed	**956km/h (594mph)**
Cruising speed	**924km/h (574mph)**
Ceiling	**10,180m (33,400ft)**
Range	**7,415km (4,000 miles)**
Flight deck crew	**Three**
Passengers	**up to 380**
First flown	**29 August 1970 (Prototype)**
Into service	**5 August 1971 (DC-10-10)**

McDonnell Douglas
MD-11

Long-range, tri-turbofan wide-body airliner

A downturn in the airline industry in the early 1980s delayed plans that McDonnell Douglas had for an improved version of the DC-10. Eventually launched in 1986, the first MD-11 flew in January 1990. Externally similar to the DC-10, the fuselage of the MD-11 is 5.7m longer. As well as various improved engine options, other modifications included a revised tail shape, the addition of winglets, upgraded flight deck and a re-designed passenger cabin. Finnair became the launch customer for the MD-11, and Italian airline Alitalia placed an order for the MD-11C 'Combi' version. However, design changes were required when the MD-11's performance did not meet expectations, and this affected sales. Other versions produced were the MD-11C/F convertible passenger/freight and extended-range MD-11ER. As with the MD-80/90 series, Boeing decided to end MD-11 production after its merger with McDonnell Douglas, the last aircraft being delivered in 2001. Of the 200 MD-11s produced, most were built as MD-11F pure freighters. In the United States, cargo carriers Federal Express and United Parcel Service (UPS) operate large fleets of MD-11s (58 and 31 respectively).

McDonnell Douglas MD-11

Engines	Three Pratt & Whitney PW4460 turbofans
Power	60,000lb thrust
Span	51.7m (169ft 6in)
Length	61.6m (202ft 0in)
Height	17.65m (57ft 9in)
Max weight	273,310kg (602,500lb)
Top speed	946km/h (588mph)
Cruising speed	930km/h (578mph)
Ceiling	12,801m (42,000ft)
Range	12,270km (7,624 miles)
Flight deck crew	Two
Passengers	up to 410
First flown	10 January 1990
Into service	December 1990

Saab
340
Twin-turboprop regional airliner

Saab
340

Twin-turboprop regional airliner

The Saab 340, initially developed as the SF340, was a joint project between Swedish manufacturer Saab and Fairchild in the United States. Under their agreement, Saab was responsible for the fuselage, with Fairchild producing the wings, engine nacelles and tail unit. Final assembly took place at the Saab factory in Sweden. The first aircraft flew at the beginning of 1983 and Crossair became the launch customer the following year. Saab assumed complete control of the 340 programme in November 1985 when Fairchild sold its interest. One of the first turboprop 30-seat regional airliners, the 340 offered new levels of passenger comfort. The 340 and similar 340A remained in production until September 1989, when they were replaced by the improved 340B. This version had more powerful engines, increased tail span and offered greater range with a higher take-off weight. The 340B Plus had an improved, quieter cabin, and extended wings for better performance. Deliveries of the 340B Plus began in September 1994. Production ended in 1998 after 430 aircraft had been built. The 340 was popular with regional airlines in the USA, and both American Eagle Airlines and Mesaba Airlines operated large fleets until 2004.

Statistics

Saab 340B Plus

Engines	**Two General Electric CT7-9B turboprops**
Power	**1,870shp**
Span	**21.44m (70ft 4in)**
Length	**19.73m (64ft 9in)**
Height	**6.97m (22ft 10in)**
Max weight	**13,155m (29,000lb)**
Top speed	**523km/h (325mph)**
Cruising speed	**467km/h (290mph)**
Ceiling	**9,450m (31,000ft)**
Range	**1,551km (964 miles)**
Flight deck crew	**Two**
Passengers	**37**
First flown	**25 January 1983 (Prototype)**
Into service	**15 June 1984 (340A)**

Saab
2000
Twin-turboprop regional airliner

HB-IZH

DARWIN AIRLINE

Saab
2000
Twin-turboprop regional airliner

The 50-seat Saab 2000, developed from the 340 and flown in March 1992, entered airline service in 1994. Faster, longer and more economical than the 340, the 2000 was powered by a pair of Allison turboshafts driving six-bladed Dowty propellers. In addition to its fuselage stretch of 7.55m, the 2000 has a 15 per cent increase in wingspan over the 340. The updated flight deck includes an Engine Indication and Crew Alert System (EICAS) and a Traffic alert and Collision Avoidance System (TCAS). The active noise control system fitted in the passenger cabin, developed for the Saab 2000, was also used in the 340B Plus from 1996. The Saab 2000 is one of the fastest turboprops flying, with a cruising speed of around 600km/h, making it comparable to some jet airliners. Despite this, sales were not strong enough to keep the 2000 in production, mainly due to the availability of the cheaper Embraer ERJ and Bombardier CRJ regional jets, and the line closed in 1999 after 60 had been built. Launch customer Crossair at one time operated 34 2000s, and over 50 remain in service, all with European airlines.

Saab 2000

Engines	**Two Allison AE 2100A turboprops**
Power	**4,125shp**
Span	**24.76m (81ft 3in)**
Length	**27.28m (89ft 6in)**
Height	**7.73m (25ft 4in)**
Max weight	**22,800kg (50,270lb)**
Top speed	**682km/h (424mph)**
Cruising speed	**594km/h (369mph)**
Ceiling	**9,450m (31,000ft)**
Range	**2,868km (1,782 miles)**
Flight deck crew	**Two**
Passengers	**50**
First flown	**26 March 1992**
Into service	**Late 1994**

Shorts
360
Twin-turboprop regional airliner

Shorts
360
Twin-turboprop regional airliner

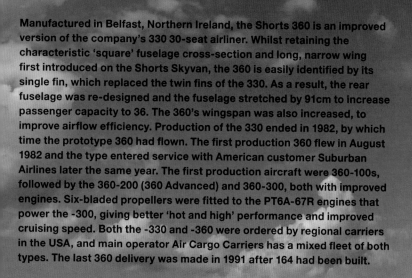

Manufactured in Belfast, Northern Ireland, the Shorts 360 is an improved version of the company's 330 30-seat airliner. Whilst retaining the characteristic 'square' fuselage cross-section and long, narrow wing first introduced on the Shorts Skyvan, the 360 is easily identified by its single fin, which replaced the twin fins of the 330. As a result, the rear fuselage was re-designed and the fuselage stretched by 91cm to increase passenger capacity to 36. The 360's wingspan was also increased, to improve airflow efficiency. Production of the 330 ended in 1982, by which time the prototype 360 had flown. The first production 360 flew in August 1982 and the type entered service with American customer Suburban Airlines later the same year. The first production aircraft were 360-100s, followed by the 360-200 (360 Advanced) and 360-300, both with improved engines. Six-bladed propellers were fitted to the PT6A-67R engines that power the -300, giving better 'hot and high' performance and improved cruising speed. Both the -330 and -360 were ordered by regional carriers in the USA, and main operator Air Cargo Carriers has a mixed fleet of both types. The last 360 delivery was made in 1991 after 164 had been built.

Shorts 360-300

Engines	Two Pratt & Whitney Canada PT6A-67R turboprops
Power	1,424shp
Span	22.80m (74ft 10in)
Length	21.58m (70ft 10in)
Height	7.27m (23ft 10in)
Max weight	12,292kg (27,100lb)
Top speed	426km/h (265mph)
Cruising speed	352km/h (219mph)
Range	745km (463 miles)
Flight deck crew	Two
Passengers	36
First flown	1 June 1981 (Prototype)
Into service	November 1982 (360-100)

Tupolev
Tu-154

Medium-range, tri-turbofan jet airliner

Tupolev
Tu-154

Medium-range, tri-turbofan jet airliner

The Tupolev Tu-154 second-generation jet was built as a replacement for the earlier Tu-104 turbojet, the Soviet Union's first jet airliner. The Tu-154 has a similar layout to the DH Trident and Boeing 727, with three rear-mounted engines and a T-tail. Designed to also replace the An-10 and Il-18 turboprops, the Tu-154 was required to operate from unprepared and rough-field airstrips. First flown in 1968, it was the first Soviet airliner not to feature a glazed nose. Its double-bogey undercarriage retracts into pods on the wings. Initial versions were powered by Kuznetsov NK-8 turbofans, but these were replaced by quieter and more economical Soloviev (now Aviadvigatel) D-30KU engines when the Tu-154M was introduced in 1984. This became the main production variant with around 400 built. Substantial numbers were ordered by Aeroflot and they became the standard medium-range airliner on routes across the Soviet Union. Several were supplied to the state airlines of Bulgaria, Hungary and Romania. The last of over 900 Tu-154s was delivered in 2002 and many remain in use by airlines in the states of the former Soviet Union.

Statistics

Tupolev Tu-154M

Engines	**Three Aviadvigatel (Soloviev) D-30KU-154 turbofans**
Power	**23,380lb thrust**
Span	**37.55m (123ft 3in)**
Length	**47.90m (157ft 2in)**
Height	**11.40m (37ft 5in)**
Max weight	**102,000kg (224,870lb)**
Top speed	**950km/h (590mph)**
Cruising speed	**900km/h (560mph)**
Ceiling	**12,100m (39,700ft)**
Range	**3,900km (2,400 miles)**
Flight deck crew	**Three/four**
Passengers	**180**
First flown	**4 October 1968 (Prototype)**
Into service	**February 1972 (Tu-154-100)**

Yakovlev
Yak-42
Short/medium-range, tri-turbofan airliner

RA-42440

Yakovlev
Yak-42

Short/medium-range, tri-turbofan airliner

Yak-42

The tri-jet Yak-40, able to seat up to 27 passengers, was the first civil transport to be designed by the Yakovlev design bureau and first flew in October 1966. It was built as a replacement for very old Lisunov Li-2 and Ilyushin Il-12/14 propeller airliners flown by the state airline Aeroflot. The three rear-mounted engines gave the small Yak-40 good short-field performance and the ability to take-off and climb on any two engines. This was important, as the aircraft would be required to fly to remote areas of the USSR. Over 1,000 were built (the majority for Aeroflot) and very few were exported to the West. Production ended in 1978. In March 1975, Yakovlev flew the Yak-42 prototype. Almost twice the length of its predecessor, the wide-body Yak-42 could seat up to 120 passengers. The three high-bypass turbofans, whilst adopting the same layout as the Yak-40, generated 50% more power. Another design change was the adoption of a 23-degree wing sweep, other new features including double-bogey landing gear, integral steps and an auxiliary power unit (APU). Over 180 were built, of which 130 are still in service.

Yakovlev Yak-42D

Engines	Three Progress ZMKB D-36 turbofans
Power	14,310lb thrust
Span	34.88m (114ft 5in)
Length	36.38m (119ft 4in)
Height	9.83m (32ft 3in)
Max weight	57,000kg (125,660lb)
Top speed	810km/h (503mph)
Cruising speed	750km/h (466mph)
Ceiling	9,600m (31,500ft)
Range	2,200km (1,367 miles)
Flight deck crew	Two or three
Passengers	120
First flown	7 March 1975 (Yak-42 prototype)
Into service	Late 1980 (Yak-42)

Yak-42

Yak-40

Checklist

Aérospatiale/BAC
Concorde
Date **Location**

Airbus
A300
Date **Location**

Airbus
A320
Date **Location**

Airbus
A330
Date **Location**

Airbus
A340
Date **Location**

Airbus
A380
Date **Location**

Antonov
An-24
Date **Location**

Avions de Transport Regional
ATR 42
Date **Location**

Boeing
707
Date **Location**

Boeing
727
Date **Location**

Boeing
737
Date   **Location**

Boeing
747
Date   **Location**

Boeing
757
Date   **Location**

Boeing
767
Date   **Location**

Boeing
777
Date   **Location**

Bombardier/Canadair
CRJ
Date   **Location**

Bombardier/DHC
Dash 8
Date   **Location**

British Aerospace
BAe 146/Avro RJ
Date   **Location**

British Aerospace
Jetstream 31
Date   **Location**

British Aerospace
Jetstream 41
Date   **Location**

Britten Norman
Islander
Date   **Location**

CASA
212
Date   Location

De Havilland Canada
Twin Otter
Date   Location

Dornier
328
Date   Location

Douglas
DC-3 Dakota
Date   Location

Douglas
DC-4 Skymaster
Date   Location

Douglas
DC-8
Date   Location

Embraer
Brasilia
Date   Location

Embraer
ERJ-145
Date   Location

Embraer
E170
Date   Location

Fairchild/Swearingen
Metro
Date   Location

Fokker
F.27 Friendship
Date   Location

Fokker
F.28 Fellowship
Date   Location

Ilyushin
Il-86
Date **Location**

Let
L-410 Turbolet
Date **Location**

Lockheed
TriStar
Date **Location**

McDonnell Douglas
DC-9
Date **Location**

McDonnell Douglas
MD-80
Date **Location**

McDonnell Douglas
DC-10
Date **Location**

McDonnell Douglas
MD-11
Date **Location**

Saab
340
Date **Location**

Saab
2000
Date **Location**

Shorts
360
Date **Location**

Tupolev
Tu-154
Date **Location**

Yakovlev
Yak-42
Date **Location**

Look out for the other
Top Trumps Books